Britannia Rules the Cut

The Royal Navy's Canal Fleet

ANDY WOOD

First Published 2009 by Appin Press, an imprint of Countyvise Limited.
14 Appin Road, Birkenhead, CH41 9HH

The right of Andy Wood to be identified as the author of this work has been asserted by him in accordance with the Copyright, Design and Patents Act 1988. Some of the material in this book was first published in the December 2008 edition of 'Canal Boat' magazine.

British Library Cataloguing in Publication Data.
A catalogue record for this book is available from the British Library.

ISBN 978 1 906205 26 3

CONTENTS

Page

Foreword

Bibliography and sources

Foreword

It all began with a photograph used as a filler in the June 2008 edition of RE:PORT, the magazine of the Boat Museum Society (BMS) at Ellesmere Port. It showed an unwieldy-looking, four metre long 'aircraft carrier', flying the Stars and Stripes, being paddled along by two men, and was accompanied by a brief paragraph which read, *"As you can tell, this strange craft comes from the USA, but it reminded the Editor of the Royal Navy 'submarine' and 'destroyer' that used to cruise the inland waterways in the 1970s. Does anyone have any information about or photographs of them?"*

One of the first to respond was Terry Waldron, an ex-Navy man, BMS member and boat-owner who proved, in the next few months, to be an assiduous researcher without whose help progress would have been very much slower. It was Terry who established that there had been four RN replica warships. The waterways writer and photographer Harry Arnold then contributed the information that the boats had all been built by the firm of John Pinder & Son. Over the following three months it was my privilege and pleasure to be in correspondence with, and to talk by telephone or face-to-face, with numerous and varied individuals who were in very many instances able to give me invaluable information and reminiscences about the Royal Navy Canal Fleet.

Although there are, frustratingly, a few loose ends still to be tied up, I owe the fact that I have been able to tell the greater part of the story in this book to the kindness, generosity and enthusiasm shown by the people and organisations listed at the back of the book. To each and every one of them, my sincere thanks.

Andy Wood

1.

Whys and Wherefores

To understand how and why the Royal Navy came to operate a fleet of scaled-down replica warships on the inland waterways, it is necessary to appreciate the wider political and military context in which such a seemingly odd activity took place.

After the Second World War Great Britain was economically – and its population emotionally and physically – exhausted. The combination of the decline of the British Empire (none too subtly encouraged by a United States riding its moral high horse) and the continuing economic hardship being experienced in Britain brought about a reduction in the size and capability of the Royal Navy. The increasingly powerful US military assumed the former role of the British, of keeping the global peace. At the same time, however, the growing threat of the Soviet Union and its Warsaw Pact allies, together with ongoing British commitments around the world made new demands on the Navy.

In the post-war era, the 1960s represented the peak of the Royal Navy's capabilities. The fleet carriers, HMS *Ark Royal*, the rebuilt HMS *Victorious* HMS *Hermes* and *HMS Centaur* gave the Royal Navy the most powerful fleet of aircraft carriers outside the United States (strange as it may seem, it was not until 1975 that the dying USSR launched its first true aircraft carrier). The Royal Navy also had a large fleet of frigates and destroyers. New more modern ships like the County class destroyers and Leander class frigates had also begun to enter service in the 1960s.

In the same decade, the Royal Navy received its first nuclear weapons and later, after the phasing-out of the RAF's V-Bombers, took on the responsibility for the UK's nuclear deterrent, to be delivered by Polaris missiles bought from the Americans and launched from a fleet of nuclear powered submarines based on an American design.

*Dennis Healey
MP, Secretary of Defence in the
Labour Government.*

Plans for the replacement of the Navy's fleet of aircraft carriers were also drawn up in the mid-1960s. Designated 'CVA-01A', the plan was to build three large aircraft carriers, each displacing about 60,000 tons, which would be able to operate the newest aircraft that were coming into service, and to maintain the United Kingdom's ranking as a major naval power. However, Dennis Healey, the Minister of Defence in the second-term Labour government, that was returned to power with a significantly larger majority in February 1966, had a mandate to cut defence spending, and the 'Queen Elizabeth' class carrier project was immediately cancelled. The Sea Lords were also ordered to scrap the existing carriers by 1971. Although the carrier, HMS *Ark Royal* was given a temporary reprieve, and lasted until 1978, this made no real difference to the overall direction of defence policy.

One of the effects, of what appeared to the British public to be the downsizing of the Navy, was seen in the decline in recruitment and the retention of experienced members of the service. In fact, the introduction of the Polaris armed submarine fleet meant that the Navy's manpower strength of roughly 98,000 would need to increase to 103,000. In 1963-64, the planned intake of recruits was 8,000, but the target was missed by about 500 men. There were at that time 180 ships in commission. In 1965 questions were asked in Parliament about the naval strength required to maintain a British presence 'East of Suez'. That year there was a shortfall of 1,000 in recruitment and retention of existing manpower was still insufficient. The shortage of aircrew for the Fleet Air Arm was 20%.

In 1966 a land-based Naval Presentation Team was formed to improve public relations and recruitment and began its first

UK tour. Re-engagement and recruiting numbers were still in decline: the reason was obvious, not only were recruiting figures down but in retention only 49% of those completing 12 years service were re-engaged although the target was 65%, and of those completing 9 years service the re-engagement of 50% was required, but only 21% was achieved.

In 1967 Naval deployments were increased to counter and to carry out surveillance of Soviet activities. The standing Beira patrol off Mozambique, designed to prevent the supply of oil and other raw materials to Ian Smith's white minority government in Rhodesia, was also still being maintained. Extensive unplanned deployments in view of political unrest in various parts of the world included that at Hong Kong provided by HMS *Bulwark* during a local strike coupled with unrest in mainland China. HMS *Hermes* also landed troops to assist the civil power in Hong Kong. Recruitment and retention continued to decline.

By 1969 the intake requirements were still not being met; that for officers was 20% below target and for ratings 30%. This was described in Parliament as a "grave situation recognised as requiring remedial action". Clearly the Naval Presentation Team was not having the hoped-for effect and things would not be helped by the decision to end the payment of re-engagement grants: another possible disincentive was the abolition of the 'Tot', the traditional rum ration on 31st July 1970!

It was probably in 1971 that the Director of Naval Recruitment met a small team from the Centre for Official Information (COI) which is, in effect, the in-house publicity and advertising agency for the Government. (Tony Murphy, a former Royal Navy Warrant Officer, confirmed to the author that the boats came under the aegis of the Director of Naval Recruiting, and that the strategy was indeed intended to boost recruitment by having a RN presence in inland towns and cities.) At the meeting the Director explained the problem of the inexorable decline in recruitment and retention of Royal Navy personnel, and asked for suggestions as to how the trend could

The CVA 01A aircraft carrier design which fell victim to defence cuts announced by Dennis Healey, the Labour Minister of Defence, in February 1966. [Photo: RN]

HMS Sheffield, now renamed Woodbine and belonging to Jean and John Moore. [Photo: Jean Moore]

Horninglow Basin, Burton-on-Trent. John Pinder's boatyard was situated out of the picture on the right; a new road has obliterated the original buildings [Photo: Rod Johnson, Creative Commons]

The aircraft carrier HMS Victorious. [Photo: RN]

A Handley-Page Victor B2, one of the three 'V Bomber' types; the others were the Avro Vulcan and the Vickers Valiant. [Photo: RAF]

be reversed. He wanted a workable plan, with costings, as soon as possible.

For their part the COI team wanted to know where the Navy recruited at present, what budget had been allocated to the exercise and what Navy resources they could call on. In rapid order, the Director rapped out the answers. As it always had, the Navy drew its recruits almost exclusively from port cities like Portsmouth, Plymouth, Bristol, Liverpool, Belfast and Glasgow, and from towns on the coast or river estuaries. As for money and other resources, within reason they could ask for whatever they needed and he would do his best to see that they got it.

At their next meeting with the Director of Recruiting the creative types from the COI had come up with a plan. They knew from their research that most of the country's ports were visited, as often as could be arranged, by warships. Where a particular ship had been 'adopted' by a port the ship would make visits and welcome aboard civic leaders and school and college parties. (An example of this was HMS *Bristol* (Pennant Number D23) which was the only Type 82 destroyer to have been built. Ironically, she had been intended as the first of the class of new large destroyers, designed specifically to escort the CVA-01A aircraft carriers, mentioned earlier. *Bristol* turned out to be a unique ship because the rest of the Type 82 class was cancelled when the CVA-01A carriers were axed as part of the 1966 Strategic Defence Review. The ship was actually commissioned at Avonmouth, the modern port of Bristol, the first Royal Navy ship to commission there, and began a lasting connection with the city.) The COI team proposed that the Directorate of Naval Recruiting should commission the building of a fleet of miniaturised warships which, by using the inland waterways, could make dramatic appearances in many inland towns and cities.

One can imagine the Director's first reaction being one of incredulity. Imray's 10 miles to the inch 'Map of the Inland Waterways of England and Wales' was no doubt spread out on the table as well as British Waterways' schematic guides to the canals. Perhaps, faced with the evidence that it was indeed possible to navigate to York, Leeds, Bradford, Manchester, Chester, Sheffield, Nottingham, Wolverhampton, Birmingham, Leicester, Oxford and London, not to mention dozens of smaller towns, the Director then turned to the question of where they proposed obtaining the boats and crews, how many boats they were suggesting should be built and exactly how much it was all going to cost.

In view of the extent of the inland waterways system, and the speed limit for boats of 4 mph, it would make sense to have at least two boats, although four would be ideal as it would give more flexibility and enable them to cover more of the system. Costs would depend on the degree of sophistication of the designs and the materials used, although using steel hulls was recommended because it would make the boats more robust. As for the crews, well, the Navy seemed the obvious place to look. The Director probably pointed out at this stage that it was the shortage of manpower that was the problem, and that the Navy couldn't just rustle up a couple of dozen sailors from nowhere, any more than he could lay his hands on vast sums of money to build the boats.

Somehow or other, however, the Director of Naval Recruiting did manage to wangle the funding to go ahead with the plan. The Directorate had agreed to order two 'sail-away' steel hulls, initially, from John Pinder & Son, a firm of boat-builders based at that time at Horninglow Basin at Burton-on-Trent. John Pinder himself recalls being contacted by what he describes as "an exhibition contractor", which in all likelihood was the COI. Savings would be made by having the final fitting out done not by Pinder's but at a reduced rate at a British Waterways yard. John Pinder would be able to obtain Thornycroft diesel engines, which he favoured for most boats that he built, from the manufacturers at a good price. The order for the first two boats was placed in the autumn of 1972, and John Pinder was supplied with drawings indicating the distinctive shapes of the boats' bows, based on the bow profiles of the ships they were designed to resemble.

John Pinder's father, Leslie had started boat building in 1946, initially converting a former torpedo boat into a cruising yacht. John joined him in 1955 and set up the company of J L Pinder and Son. In the early days the company, which was based at Horninglow Basin in Burton-on-Trent, repaired and conserved working boats but, in the late '60s, with the increasing leisure use of the canals, John developed an all-welded steel narrowboat in a cruising style and the company moved into the market for privately owned boats.

The company had to leave Burton when a new road was planned which would require the demolition of its buildings and would drastically reduce the size of the basin, and moved to Hopwood on the Coventry Canal (although since 1987 it has been based on a site in Stoke Prior). The Pinder name was, and is, associated with versatility and quality, building ocean-going vessels, sailing vessels and bespoke vessels like 90ft barges. It must have been those qualities that brought the firm the Royal Navy contract. John Pinder was originally given to understand that, in total, the Navy would require five boats (later reduced to four) of which, in order to spread the cost over two Financial Years, the second pair were to be delivered in 1973, with payment for them not falling due until the April.

It had been decided that the first two boats would resemble, as far as possible, one of the nuclear-powered Polaris missile-armed submarines, known to Jacks as 'bomber boats', and very much the symbol of the Navy's status as the guardian of the British nuclear deterrent. HMS *Renown* (Pennant Number S26) was the identity that was chosen for this boat. The first of the surface ships whose identity was to be borrowed was the 'County' class guided missile destroyer, HMS *London* (Pennant Number D16) which had been commissioned in 1963.

When completely fitted out, the replica HMS *Renown*, built at Horninglow, was 60 feet (18.29 metres) long with a beam of 6 feet 10 inches (2.08 metres) and displaced about 20 tons (20.2 tonnes) compared with the real submarine (commissioned

in 1968) which was 425 ft (130 metres) long, with a beam of
33 ft (10 metres) and which displaced 7,500 tons (7,620 tonnes)
when surfaced and 8,400 tons (8,535) when submerged. (Is there
any need to add that the replica was not capable of submerging
– at least, not deliberately?). The replica HMS *London,* built at
Hopwood, was also 60 feet by 6 feet 10 inches and similarly
displaced some 20 tons, while the original ship displaced 6,800
tons (6,909) fully fuelled and armed and was 521.5 feet (158.9
metres) long with a beam of 54 ft (16.4 metres).

The boats left the yards where they were built as 'sail
aways', that is capable of cruising under their own power, but
otherwise being bare shells consisting of nothing more than
the hull and a basic cabin, for which John Pinder charged the
Ministry of Defence £7,000 apiece. *London* left Hopwood in
September 1971 to cruise to the British Waterways yard at
Bulls Bridge, at the junction of the Grand Union Canal and the
Paddington Arm in London: it was followed to Bulls Bridge,
in February 1972, by *Renown.* John Pinder recalls that "at the
time the first one was due to go, the Grand Union (Canal) was
closed, so I approached the Thames Conservancy for a passage
from Oxford to Brentford, for which they obliged by sending a
free passage document, stating the owners as 'The Royal Navy'
and the vessel type as 'County Class Destroyer'. The looks we
had off the Lock Keepers were hilarious!"

The British Waterways staff at Bulls Bridge had to have
both boats fully fitted and ready for use by 1st April, as it had
been decided that they would tour the waterways for six months
of the year, finishing at the end of September. They set about
transforming the boats into convincing replicas of warships with
a will – it certainly made a change from carrying out repairs
to BW's own working boats. Creating a reasonably accurate
replica of the destroyer was relatively straightforward, but the
rounded nose of the submarine had to be formed from marine
ply with taped seams, bent over a soft wood frame.

Meanwhile a lot of thought had been going into the question of who was to crew the boats and who was to be in overall charge of the fleet.

A Polaris missile at the Science Museum. [Photo: John Griffiths, Creative Commons]

2.

Officers and Men

Of course, it was true that an overall shortage of manpower
in the Navy was a problem, rather than a solution to the matter
of crewing the canal boats; however, the most people the canal
fleet would ever need in any one year would be, say, sixteen
ratings and four more senior men to captain the boats – not
officers, but Petty Officers or Leading Rates. Whoever had
overall command responsibility would clearly have to be an
officer, and he would need a lieutenant and perhaps a couple
of Jennies to do the office work; twenty-one people in all. But
where to get them from? This was where a bit of lateral thinking
was required.

Royal Navy officers joined for a first commission of twelve
years (Royal Marine officers for eight years). Ratings joined up
either for nine or twelve years. Both officers and ratings could,
if they wished, sign on for a further period of service; this is
what is meant by the term 'retention'. Just to confuse matters,
when in active use, Royal Navy ships are also 'commissioned'.
Routinely, in peacetime ships return to port in the United
Kingdom for periodic refits during which they undergo thorough
maintenance and repair and may have additional weapons or
instrument systems fitted. Inevitably, there will be some officers
and ratings, whose remaining period of service is not much more
than a year, and who would therefore be unlikely to be sent
abroad on another ship. They would usually be given shore-
based jobs in offices or stores. It would certainly be possible to
muster enough men for a total complement of twenty-one.

Obviously, the Directorate of Naval Recruiting would need
a reasonably senior and experienced officer to have overall
command of the canal fleet. Fortunately, Lieutenant-Commander
James Green the captain of the boom defence vessel HMS

Barfoil, based in Singapore, had just been ordered home and had about eighteen months left to serve. Most recently, *Barfoil* had been a regular sight in Singapore dockyard maintaining the boom defence during the small, undeclared war that had flared, from 1962 to 1966, between Indonesia and Malaysia which involved Commonwealth forces from Australia, New Zealand and Great Britain, as well as from the newly declared Federation of Malaysia. Accordingly, Lieutenant-Commander Green was ordered to report to the Directorate, where he was apprised of his new responsibilities.

'Jimmy' Green, as he became affectionately known by the men under his command, was a short man, by then tending to stoutness, and is said to have been "a real gentleman". He was certainly no martinet; in fact he seems to have had an impish sense of humour. More than one of the Canal Fleet crewmen recall that, although he spent most of his time in the office back in London, from time to time he would appear unannounced on the towpath, 'just checking'.

In 1972, when there was just the one pair of boats, day to day command was exercised by Fleet Chief Petty Officer Alfred 'Harry' Tate, a genial Scots senior warrant officer, who inspired the devotion of his men by his good humour and fairness: he was the sort of NCO that the ratings didn't want to let down.

As for the ratings and marines, the Directorate circulated details of the work of the Canal Fleet quite widely and took its pick of those who, either, had obtained permission from their commanding officers to volunteer, or had been 'volunteered' by them. In the latter case, they were not always aware of what the posting would entail. For example, in March 1974 Mike Dowling, a Leading Marine Engineering Mechanic, was given an order to report to Old Admiralty Arches in London. He was told that he was to be part of a new recruitment campaign but, other than that, the only detail he was given was the date on which he was to report for duty - 1st April.

"Considering the date I was to arrive", he recalls "...the complete lack of joining instructions and the lack of any other information, I was very sceptical, to say the least".

However, an order is an order. When he reported for duty, the mystery deepened: he was told that he would be joining his next ship, not at Portsmouth or Chatham, but at a boatyard on the Grand Union Canal. It's easy to imagine his shock when the ship turned out to resemble a nuclear submarine no more than 60 feet long and 6 feet 10 inches wide!

As far as can be ascertained, command of the Canal Fleet remained unchanged for the second year, with Lieutenant Commander Green at Admiralty Arch and FCPO Tate with the boats. They had evidently been appointed full time to the staff of the Directorate of Recruiting.

Eric Reeves served on HMS *Renown* for six months in 1973 as a Leading Hand. That year, the day to day command of the boats - *Renown* was paired with *Sheffield* - was again the responsibility of FCPO Tate, as it had been the previous year. Eric remembers his time on *Renown* with great affection and he describes Harry Tate as 'a proper gentleman'. He also remembers that the money was good; because he was married he qualified for separation money, and in addition the crews were paid a subsistence allowance, which was rarely needed since they either slept aboard the boats, or sometimes were put up on the premises of the local Sea Cadet Corps.

Renown had four bunks and *Sheffield* had two bunks and two camp beds, and both boats were equipped with small cookers and sinks. One correspondent says, "The layout of the boats was very ingenious... The living accommodation [such as it was] was hidden behind the panelling." For power, the boats had electrical generators as well as the diesel engines. Usually the two boats would moor stem to stern and Eric would rig up a cable from *Renown* to *Sheffield* so that electricity for both only needed one generator running.

Life aboard was rather crowded with five men to a boat, so the Fleet Chief had brought in an arrangement, whereby each man in rotation was given a week's home leave. On one occasion this resulted in a returning member of the crew arriving back at the boats in a police car.

It happened like this: the rating had been told to rejoin *Renown* at Dudley in the West Midlands. He duly arrived in the town but had no idea where the canal was. Presenting himself at the front desk of the police station, he told the desk Sergeant that he was looking for a submarine and asked him where he might find it. In a world-weary voice, the Sergeant asked, "Had a drink have we, sir?" Finally persuaded that the rating was sober and serious, he put out a call and soon learnt that a patrol had located *Renown* and *Sheffield* moored near Dudley Zoo. The police gave the relieved rating a lift to the boats where a similarly disillusioned FCPO Tate had to be convinced that the rating had not disgraced the Andrew (one of the terms by which the Royal Navy is known) by being taken into police custody.

A six month posting to the inland waterways fleet seems to have been regarded as something of a holiday, particularly by the ratings, despite the fact that sometimes, when two destinations were quite far apart, they might have to be ready for action at first light and be on the move until after dark. (The boats were fitted with navigation lights and spotlights.) As a rule, the crews, warrant officers and ratings alike, were on first name terms, although they reverted to "aye, aye, sir" when members of the public were present.

In 1974 it seems that Jimmy Green had retired, because a Lieutenant O'Brien was in overall command, (he would be succeeded by Lieutenant Commander Charles Gidley Wheeler in 1975 and Lieutenant Commander P A Voûte in 1976, both former Fleet Air Arm pilots.)

Each member of the crew was issued with a lock key, or windlass, and a spare in case they lost one. However, they had to pay for any that could not be found. On one occasion, when the boats were on the move, there was a loud splash as somebody went into the canal.

When the man surfaced the others called out, "What happened? Did you trip up?" "No," he replied, "I dropped my ****** lock key. So I jumped in to see if I cold find it; I'm ****** if I'm going to pay for it!"

Photographs taken in 1974 show a different FCPO, although with a 'full set' beard similar to Harry Tate's, apparently in charge of *Renown* and *Cleopatra*. (Sad to relate, Harry Tate died of cancer in service the following year.)

On another occasion the boats, not unusually, were tied up next to a pub and, naturally, the crews went for a few jars. Afterwards, feeling quite 'relaxed' they sat on the aft deck chatting. One of the lads was showing off a gold-plated cigarette lighter that his girl friend had given him, when it slipped from his fingers, bounced off the deck and disappeared beneath the water. They tried to retrieve it but without success. We don't know for sure what the young lady said when he confessed, but we can guess that she wasn't best pleased!

Neil Duffy, who has a unique distinction connected with the Canal Fleet (which is explained in a later chapter) contributes the following story: "I can remember meeting up with them in the wilds of the Leeds & Liverpool Canal. I think it was at 'The Anchor' at Salterforth between Colne and Skipton. I had been fishing up there with a colleague. The crews told us that it used to raise a laugh, when they walked into a lonely canalside pub. The locals couldn't work out how their tap room was suddenly full of Royal Navy ratings; 'Where've you lot come from then?' they'd ask."

Perhaps the best story, because of the wonderful image it conjures up, is of a destroyer and a nuclear submarine going hell for leather down the River Severn. As all of the boats were powered by the same size engines, any attempt to race each other would usually result in a dead heat. However, on this occasion Eric Reeves disappeared into *Renown*'s engine room and uncoupled the governor that limited the speed of the engine. *Renown* then drew majestically and inexorably ahead of *Sheffield*, while her crew waved a mocking goodbye to their oppos on the slower boat.

Admiralty Arch flying the White Ensign, the flag of the Royal Navy. [Photo: Jack Tsen-Ta Lee]

Jacks on parade. [Photo: RN]

3.

Creating the Illusion

The sail-away boats that John Pinder & Son Ltd delivered to Bulls Bridge in London looked like very plain narrowboats, with severely angular cabins completely without windows. It was the job of the skilled craftsmen at the British Waterways (BW) boatyard at Bulls Bridge to transform them, internally and externally, into convincing replicas of warships many times their size.

We can gain a detailed insight into what this involved, thanks to an illustrated article in 'Waterways News', BWB's house journal, published in May 1973, (unearthed by Colin Edmondson of the River Weaver Society, and also a member of the Boat Museum Society).

"Last year the Royal Navy made its debut on the inland waterways with two 60ft long, specially built boats cruising the rivers and canals of Great Britain. The superstructure of the boats was designed to resemble a Polaris submarine and a guided missile destroyer. A third boat a Leander class frigate joined them towards the end of last year. 1973 sees the fourth boat, a type 42 destroyer joining the fleet to start another season cruising on the inland waterways appearing at rallies and water festivals all over the country."

The caption to a photograph of the highly detailed interior of Renown read: "With a hidden tape recorder already installed playing convincing sounding asdic 'pings' it only needs someone to shout 'dive, dive' and visitors to this replica Polaris submarine could well imagine they will be taken on a 'voyage to the bottom of the canal' The photograph shows the inside of HMS Renown, with a member of the Royal Navy ready to show visitors to the canal fleet how this intricate panel of dials works."

HMS Renown at Little Venice. The casing, or upper hull, was made of marine ply shaped in a steam box at the BW yard at Bulls Bridge.

HMS London receiving visitors at Little Venice. [Photo: RN]

British Waterways craftsmen fitting out HMS Renown, using instruments and fittings from decommissioned warships, at Bulls Bridge yard. [Photo: BWB]

The real HMS Cleopatra. [Photo: navyphotos.co.uk]

The real HMS London. [Photo: navyphotos.co.uk]

The real HMS Renown.
[Photo: RN]

The real HMS Sheffield,
which was lost in the
Falklands War.
[Photo: RN]

*The display aboard HMS Sheffield.
[Photo: RN]*

*HMS London and HMS
Renown at a rally at
Atherstone on the Coventry
Canal. [Photo: Peter Scott]*

*Using the periscope on HMS
Renown. FCPO Tate seated in the
background. [Photo RN]*

The article continues: "The idea behind what are probably the most unusual vessels launched by the Royal Navy since the war, is to tour the inland waterways in a publicity venture aimed at taking the Royal Navy to areas far from the sea.

"After an official launching of the submarine, HMS *Renown* and the destroyer HMS *London* at last year's Boat Afloat Show at Little Venice by members of 'The Navy Lark', the two boats covered over 1,000 miles of waterways. They went through 583 locks and 17 tunnels. The 98-year-old Anderton lift has carried a variety of boats up and down from the Trent & Mersey Canal to the Weaver Navigation, but the most unusual must have been the Navy canal fleet as they made their way to the IWA National Rally at Lymm [on the Bridgewater Canal]. Over 117,000 people visited the boats during 1972."

Another photograph accompanying the article was captioned: "Board employees at Bulls Bridge Repair Yard working on the conversion of the interior of the Polaris submarine *Renown* during the early part of this year. The maze of dials, gauges, cables and switches were installed by employees using sketches and drawings supplied by the Royal Navy. Paul Francis foreman boat builder at Bulls Bridge spent a day in Portsmouth looking around a submarine to get a mental picture of an authentic ship."

The article itself continued: "This year again under command of Lieutenant Commander James Green they hope to have an even more successful season and as an added attraction two of the boats have been fitted out inside as authentic ships. Up to now the interiors have carried a small exhibition of photographs and illuminated colour transparencies showing the role of the vessel in the Navy, the life which the men in such a ship lead and prospects in the Navy today for young men from the age of 16 upwards.

"The frigate HMS *Cleopatra* and the type 42 destroyer HMS *Sheffield* will still carry this photographic display, but the *Renown* and *London* have been fitted with instruments, dials, knobs, coloured lights and even a periscope in the sub. This 'real life' interior will give young men a chance to see what it would really be like to serve on a guided missile destroyer or a Polaris submarine with the Navy.

"Some good sales talk from Martin Japes assistant chief engineer (Engineering services) backed by the service given in 1972 by employees along the Board's system, and the support of the Board's Repair Yards to assist the tour, convinced the Navy that the work to fit out the miniature ships should be done at Bulls Bridge Repair Yard. The Repair Yard already has a contract for the fleet to be based there for the winter refit which included a complete engine overhaul. Although a variety of skilled tasks are tackled by the men at Bulls Bridge this interior installation was probably one of the most unusual. The men under Paul Francis, foreman boat builder, worked from drawings and sketches provided by the Navy. Paul had in fact spent a day at Portsmouth to look around the interior of a submarine.

"The instrument panels in the sub and destroyer all come from actual Navy ships which have been either refitted or are now out of commission. The periscope came from a wartime midget submarine. If only that conglomeration of dials and gauges from a variety of naval ships could talk, they could surely tell a salty tale or two!"

The interior of HMS Sheffield.
[Photo: BWB]

Bulls Bridge Junction between the Grand Union Canal and the Paddington Arm.

4.

Here, There and Everywhere

Thanks to Mike Dowling, who served on one of the boats and who, fortunately, preserved a copy of the official 'Royal Navy Canals Touring Exhibition' leaflet from 1974, we have a detailed list of the many venues visited by the two pairs of boats that year. The leaflet explains, "The Royal Navy's Canal Fleet of miniature warships was commissioned in April for the third year – to be spent covering some three thousand miles of canal and river systems in six months to publicise the Navy. Last year the Fleet visited some 50 cities, towns and villages and received some 200,000 visitors.

"The four craft, *Sheffield, Renown, Cleopatra* and *London*, are scaled down versions of real ships and submarines, with superstructures mounted on traditional canal narrow boat hulls. The craft, which are 60 feet long and have a beam of seven feet, are fitted inside with actual equipment used in HM Ships, thus giving the atmosphere of a front line warship." There follows a truly impressive list of dates and venues.

HMS Cleopatra on the moorings of the Retford & Worksop Boat Club. [Photo: George Stokes]

10th April	Paddington Arm, Little Venice, London
13th -15th April	Berkhamsted
20th -25th April	Farmers Bridge, Birmingham
27th -28th April	Stoke-on-Trent
4th -5th May	Evesham
11th -12th May	Worcester
18th -19th May	Oxford
25th -27th May	Slade Heath Covert, Staffordshire
1st -2nd June	Stratford-on-Avon
8th -9th June	Lincoln
15th -18th June	York
22nd -23rd June	Shipley
29th -30th June	Tamworth
6th -7th July	Foxton
13th -14th July	Newark
20th -21st July	Thorne
27th -29th July	Sheffield
3rd -4th August	Blackburn
10th -11th August	Nantwich
17th -18th August	Autherley Junction, Wolverhampton
24th -26th August	Nottingham
30th August -1st September	Abingdon
14th -15th September	Henley
17th September	Bulls Bridge

This programme would have taken them on the Grand Union Canal, the Birmingham & Fazeley Canal, the Coventry Canal, the Trent & Mersey Canal, the Birmingham Canal Navigations, the Stratford Canal, the River Trent, the Fossdyke, the River Ouse, the Selby Canal, the River Aire, the Leeds-Liverpool Canal, the River Calder, the Sheffield & South Yorkshire Canal, the Stainforth & Keadby Canal, the Soar Navigation, the Leicester Arm of the G U Canal, the Shropshire Union Canal, the Staffordshire & Worcestershire Canal, the Erewash Canal and the River Thames. Meanwhile, also starting on 10th April, *Cleopatra* and *London* had an equally busy and wide-ranging programme:

10th April	Paddington Arm, Little Venice, London
13th -15th April	Watford
20th - 21st April	Northampton
27th - 28th April	Peterborough
4th - 5th May	Wellingborough
11th -12th May	Leighton Buzzard
18th -19th May	Rickmansworth
21st May - 2nd June	Paddington Arm, Little Venice, London
8th - 10th June	Stoke Prior
15th - 16th June	Wolverhampton
22nd - 23rd June	Gloucester
29th - 30th June	Tame Valley, Birmingham
6th - 7th July	Nantwich
13th - 14th July	Stone, Staffordshire
19th 0 21st July	Tewkesbury
27th - 28th July	Chester
3rd - 4th August	Wigan
10th - 11th August	Leeds
17th - 18th August	Clayworth, near Retford
24th-27th August	Leicester
31st August - 1st September	Banbury
7th - 8th September	Stourport
14th - 15th September	Coventry
20th September	Bulls Bridge

The visit of *Cleopatra* and *London* to Little Venice from 21st May to 2nd June was for the 'Boat Afloat Show' organised by British Waterways, where the RN Canal Fleet had also been represented in the previous two years.

Fleet chief Petty Officer Harry Tate.

HMS Renown and HMS Cleopatra at Camden Lock. [Photo: Jackie Hallowes]

HMS London on the Retford & Worksop Boat Club moorings. [Photo: George Stokes]

Office Lock, Leeds. [Photo: Leeds City Council]

"I'd primed the touch-hole with powder and brought the port fire down, and off she went with a bloody good 'Bang!'... "Oh bloody hell; I'm in for it now!"

The 1974 programme leaflet noted, "The canal fleet versions of both *Cleopatra* and *Sheffield* have been completely remodelled inside during this year's refit. Between them they carry sonar, operations and communications equipment. Although this equipment is not the most modern it is still used in Royal Navy ships today".

Occasionally there were mishaps, some more dramatic than others. Brent Hinchliffe recalls, "My family and I were moored up at Farmers Bridge, Birmingham and the next boat to us was the submarine. I recall very clearly the moment they cast off on the next stage of their journey when one of the crew - I think it might have been a Petty Officer - slipped gracefully from the casing (hull) into the basin. This gave rise to some amusement among the onlookers. Interestingly my son, who was with us at the time, subsequently joined the Royal Navy and became Commander of a nuclear submarine".

This seems like an appropriate point at which to recall that, among the crews, the fleet was known affectionately as "Harry Tate's Navy", because of FCPO Tate's association with it. Originally, the term had been coined for the Royal Naval Patrol Service (RNPS), which played a vital role in the coastal defence of Britain during the Second World War. The RNPS consisted of merchant vessels crewed by civilian volunteers and conscripts. The Service's role at first was keeping the shipping lanes around the UK clear but the men of the RNPS also served in many other theatres of war.

The original Harry Tate was a Scottish comedian who performed on the music halls from before the Great War until the 1930s, and was famous for sketches in which he clumsily failed to operate various contraptions; his act included, for example, a car that gradually fell apart as he tried to repair it. Between the wars, the term 'Harry Tate' was applied to anything that was clumsy, amateurish or incompetent ("that's a bit Harry Tate'"). Subsequently, any sailor whose surname was Tate was given the nickname Harry, no matter how senior his rank.

Another civilian boater wrote: "There is a story that [the Canal Fleet's] first appearance on the Leeds & Liverpool had not been telegraphed to the staff. The lock-keeper at Office Lock in Leeds nearly had a thrombo when he saw a submarine and a destroyer rising in his lock through the toll-office window!"

In a letter to the author, Neil Michael Duffy provided the details of the only known occasion on which a vessel of the RN Canal Fleet came under hostile fire:

"I used to be a re-enactor in the Sealed Knot and also the English Civil War Society (ECWS). We were an artillery regiment with black powder, muzzle loaders, roughly a 2 oz charge, wadded; made a lovely bang when done right.

"In 1975 our regiment took under its wing a new demi-culverin, a 9lb, though some said it was a 2lb, canon. It was cast at Birstall Foundries between Leeds and Batley. In the ECWS it was a Parliamentary gun.

"Our first outing was at Brill in 1976. Now a 2 oz blank charge was not enough really for the piece, so we stepped it up. With a cast iron barrel nearly ten feet long, it took some warming up. Usually your first three or four loadings would be what we called 'flamers', just a long flame and a lot of white powder smoke. Well, once the barrel was warmed up, and with good ramming of the wadding over the charge, then she'd go. At Brill I was credited with knocking over a pike regiment over 300 yards away with the shock wave from the barrel.

"Now at some time everybody gets their comeuppance. Well, I got mine. In either '76 or '77, I forget exactly [It must have been in 1977]. A length of canal – it might have been the Cromford - was reopened, plenty of barges, narrowboats, the RN recruitment boys and us, well, a couple of pike and musketeer regiments and our demi-culverin.

"It's a Saturday in summer. We get to the place. First job is to get the canon on to the canal bank. It was complicated but we got there eventually, even after the bank gave way under the left-hand wheel, and three of us jumped into the canal to hold the wheel, and the RN lads roped up and helped us out.

"So, here comes my comeuppance. I'm on the canal bank going through the motions for the spectators and actually firing flamers, slowly warming up the barrel. I've got the canon below the line of boats, so that there is nothing in the way.

"Now a narrowboat is normally 60-70 feet long, so in a canal every so often you would find a winding hole so they could turn round. These were usually very shallow [on the far side] as only the bow would go in and you would use your engine to pull you out astern and round you went.

"It was a sultry sort of day. I was busy as I said, and I wasn't paying attention to what was moving on the canal. The Big Wig had done his job and opened the canal. The canon was fired. Resounding 'Crack!', ho, ho, ho, ox roast, beer tent, quick bite to eat, glug, glug, glug, and a blank fired every thirty minutes. Then through it all again.

"For some reason *Cleopatra* had to drop back before she could use the winding hole and turn round. I was busy. Usually you had a crew of five men on a canon; one holding the powder canister, one the powder ladle (we didn't use bagged charges), one holding the rammer, one to sponge out and one man to prime and fire. So as I was going through the motions, I wasn't noticing what was happening on the cut.

"I'd primed the touch-hole with powder and brought the port fire down, and off she went with a bloody good 'Bang!' Round the front, sponge out... "What's everybody looking at?" Turn round... "Oh bloody hell; I'm in for it now!"

"*Cleopatra* had gone astern and was in the act of turning in the winding hole. The shock wave caught her on her port side, rolled her and left her high and dry, stuck in the mud of the winding hole!

"If I remember correctly, we pulled her round with the winch on the front of our Land Rover. It cost me a lot of beers later on. It may seem far-fetched, but it did happen."

5.

"Left Hand Down A Bit"

Leslie Phillips (in the rowing boat) attempts to 'tow' HMS London and other members of the Navy Lark at the 'Boat Afloat Show' in Little Venice, 1972. [Photo: RN]

In earlier chapters there have been references to different combinations of *Renown, Sheffield, Cleopatra* and *London* taking part in the Boat Afloat Show at Little Venice in London. These appearances at the Show meant that for many people the boats of the Royal Navy Canal Fleet would always have something of the glamour of showbiz associated with them. The reason was that the boats were 'commissioned' each year by the stars of the long-running BBC radio comedy series, 'The Navy Lark'.

In 1972, 'Navy News', the house journal of the Royal Navy reported: "Six cast members of the BBC's 'Navy Lark' pitched up to take charge of HMS *London* and *Renown* at the Little Venice Boat Show Afloat in London.

"Sadly they weren't given charge of the real things, but two 60ft barges (*sic*) - the first two members of the Royal Navy's Canal Barge Fleet - which bore a striking, if scaled-down, resemblance to the County class guided missile destroyer HMS *London*, and the Polaris submarine HMS *Renown*.

"Four mini-ships were built to represent contemporary naval vessels which could then be toured around British cities and towns with inland waterways where the real thing could never reach.

"The third and fourth barges, representing a Leander class frigate and new Type 42 destroyer, were still being built at the time, and were expected to join their Canal Barge fleet later in the year.

"'Navy Lark' and real ex-Navy veteran Jon Pertwee also stopped by to visit the Navy's miniature exhibition fleet."

(It should perhaps be pointed out that the Royal Navy – and 'Navy News' – is familiar with 'barges' but not, on the whole, with 'narrowboats', so waterways enthusiasts should forgive the sacrilegious use of the term 'barge' in this context!)

"The Navy Lark", written by Laurie Wyman (and co-writer George Evans from the twelfth series), was about the misadventures of the crew of the fictional Royal Navy ship HMS *Troutbridge*. The show was first broadcast on the Light Programme in 1959 and ran for thirteen series until 1976, making it the second longest running radio programme the BBC had made up to that point. Interestingly, far from having been a Jack, Laurie Wyman had actually been in the Army making him, in Navy slang, a 'pongo' (from "where the Army goes the pong goes").

The main characters of the show were: Chief Petty Officer Pertwee, played by Jon Pertwee (later the third incarnation of Dr Who); Sub Lieutenant Phillips, played by Leslie Phillips and the Number One (First Lieutenant), who was played by Dennis Price in the first series and after that by Stephen Murray. The rest of the regular characters were played by Richard Caldicott,

Ronnie Barker, Tenniel Evans, Michael Bates and Heather Chasen.

Those of us who are of a certain age can be instantly transported back to a more innocent age by Mr Phillips' order to the helmsman, "Left hand down a bit", or by Tenniel Evans, in the persona of Leading Seaman Goldstein, calling from his starboard lookout's post to alert the bridge to the fact that the ship was approaching a hazard: "Leadin' Seaman Goldstein chattin'. I don't know whether you've noticed, sir, but we're heading straight for the harbour wall!"

It might be expected that serving members of the Royal Navy would have resented the way in which the Senior Service was represented, but far from it. The ratings loved the portrayal of officers as inept, panicky, deaf or downright stupid, after all, they habitually referred to officers as 'pigs' (and a posh sounding officer as a 'quaffer'), midshipmen as 'piglets' and, inevitably, the officers' mess as 'the pigsty'.

On the officers' side, it's a wise officer who knows the wisdom of allowing the other ranks to have a good 'drip', or moan, to get things out of their system. Certainly, the men of the Canal Fleet had no objection to sharing the limelight with Sub-Lieutenant Phillips, Lieutenant Murray, Captain Povey and CPO Pertwee (who really was a former Naval officer), particularly as there always seemed to be plenty of bikini-clad girls in the offing at the Boat Afloat Show; as Mr Phillips was wont to say, "Phwoar!"

Little Venice, where the Boat Afloat Show took place, was where the RN Canal Fleet was frequently photographed, since it was an attractive setting and not very far from the fleet's Bulls Bridge winter base. Prior to the Second World War, the area had always been called Paddington. Although the poet Robert Browning, who lived in the area from 1861 to 1868, is often credited with coining the name 'Little Venice', It was actually Lord Byron who compared it – unfavourably – with Venice, wishing that it was more like Venice than the dirty, run down place that it was at that time. It was in the Victorian era that the

Church Commissioners, who owned much of the surrounding land, encouraged the building of terraces of substantial stuccoed houses.

By the 1970s the name Little Venice had firmly attached itself to the area, and the canal junctions and the pool with its island (still known as 'Browning's Island', perpetuating the myth) obviously provided an attractive setting, easily reached by Londoners, for a boat show where many of the exhibits could be viewed afloat (as opposed to the Earl's Court boat show).

It was inevitable that bringing The Navy Lark cast together with miniature replica warships would produce some inspired lunacy. One surviving photograph shows Captain Povey on the foredeck of *London* paying out two very slender cables with which Lieutenant Phillips, sitting in a skiff assisted by a young lady, is attempting to tow the destroyer; another shows the Admiral (another of Tenniel Evans' roles) and Captain Povey (Richard Caldicott) inspecting a row of identical, lifesize, cardboard cut-out ratings at the water's edge.

Jon Pertwee (top row centre) and FCPO 'Harry' Tate (bottom row right) aboard HMS Cleopatra at Little Venice. [Photo: RN]

(Left to right) Michael Bates, Stephen Murray, Leslie Phillips, Heather Chasen, Tenniel Evans and a genuine RN officer inspecting the 'crew' of HMS London. [Photo: RN]

Browning's Pool and Island, Little Venice, c 1965.

The boom defence vessel HMS Barfoil which was Lieutenant-Commander James Green's last seagoing command before he was given overall command of the RN Canal Fleet.

*(From left) Jon Pertwee,
Leslie Phillips and Stephen
Murray in The Navy Lark.
[Photo: BBC]*

*Stephen Murray, Richard
Caldicott and Leslie Phillips in
The Navy Lark. [Photo: BBC]*

*Ronnie Barker in
The Navy Lark.*

*Spot the Actors! Members of
The Navy Lark cast mingle
with the genuine article.
Syd Harrison is second from
the left. [Photo: RN]*

6.

Hunt for Survivors

After a fair-sized tidal wave of letters and emails had brought information about the boats pouring in to the author, naturally the questions that sprang to mind were, What had happened to the boats after they were retired from 'active service' by the Royal Navy? Had any of them survived for more than thirty years? If so, who owned them and where were they now?

Very early in my attempts to find out what I could about the Royal Navy Canal Fleet, my fellow member of the Boat Museum Society, Terry Waldron, sent me a photograph that he had taken of a boat moored on the River Trent at Nottingham. Terry was convinced that it was a survivor of the Canal Fleet. At first glance it looked like an old and rather tired standard narrowboat, apart from its rather strangely shaped front end. Terry thought that it might be *Cleopatra*, the former 'frigate', but he knew for certain that it belonged to the Nottingham Sea Cadet Corps. He said he would try to contact the Commanding Officer of the Corps.

Very soon he had a reply to his enquiry, from Lieutenant Michelle Welsh, RNR, which read:

"Thank you for your enquiry regarding Cleopatra narrow boat. Nottingham Unit did own this for some years and eventually had to decide on its future. Due to funds the Unit sold Cleopatra in May [2008]. Many, many years ago the Frigate type boat was converted into a narrow boat that was hired out to Sea Cadets units up and down the Eastern Area, and I can confirm that we had great times onboard. The narrow boat then was moved to Thorne/Scunthorpe for a few years where unfortunately it got vandalised and then was taken back on by Nottingham Unit. Due to the amount of money required to update her, she was

eventually sold to a private owner. Since she has been sold there has been quite a bit of interest in her."

Many of the people who came forward with information were responding to appeals in the monthly free newspaper "Towpath Talk". One of them was Mark Ellard of Redhill Marina, Ratcliffe-on-Soar – not all that far from where the Nottingham Sea Cadets had their mooring.

"You're looking for that Royal Navy boat *Cleopatra*", he said on the phone.

"We certainly are."

"Well, I've got her. Her new owners have brought her in for sandblasting, blacking and a repaint."

Mark said that he would tell *Cleopatra*'s owners that he had spoken to me, so that they could get in touch if they wanted to.

I wondered if they would, or if they would prefer to remain anonymous, but it was only a couple of days later that Mrs Marsden rang up to say that she and her husband, together with their son, had bought the boat. She was delighted to hear that it had been part of the RN Canal Fleet. I was equally delighted to have it confirmed that at least one of the boats had survived. I promised to send as much information as I had about *Cleopatra* and a selection of photographs. Not long afterwards I had a note which read:

"Thank you very much for the photographs you sent us... When Cleopatra is finished we are going to frame them and put them on the wall with all her history."

Terry Waldron had pointed me in the direction of Jim Shead's website (www.jim-shead.com), which is possibly the most outstanding source of information about the inland waterways on the Internet, and suggested that I looked up the four RN boats on the list of boat registrations. Sure enough, there was *Cleopatra*'s entry:

CLEOPATRA, Built by ROYAL NAVY - Length: 62 feet (18.90 metres) Beam: 6 feet 6 inches (1.98 metres). Metal hull. Registered with BW, number 79572 as a powered craft.

Logic seemed to dictate that the registration of at least one of the other boats *Sheffield* which entered service the same year – should be close to *Cleopatra*'s in the list. No such luck! It was frustrating, because with all the registration numbers it would be a lot easier to trace the remaining boats, but there was no sign of *Sheffield, London* or *Renown.*

However, I wasn't entirely out of luck: "Towpath Talk" reeled in another catch. I had a phone call from a lady called Jean Moore.

"I've just read the piece in "Towpath Talk" about the Royal Navy boats," she said. "I think we're living on one of them".

If so, I wondered, which one was it? "Really? How long have you had her?"

"Six or seven years. The chap we bought her from had spent quite a bit on fitting her out, and he and his wife used to go all over the place on her. But when his wife died, he didn't have the heart to carry on and we bought her."

"What's her name?"

"She was called *Woodbine* when we got her. We quite like the name."

Jean and her husband John lived aboard *Woodbine* in a marina in Leicester. Without being asked, Jean volunteered the information that she had seen one of the boats when she was a girl, moored on the River Soar at Abbey Park. I was able to tell her that the boat she had seen was *Cleopatra* in her first season in 1973 when she made her solo visit to Leicester. I asked her if she and John had had *Woodbine* out of the water. They had, to have the bottom re-blacked, and they had taken some photos of her at the time.

From the photograph of the whole fleet I had found on the

HMS Cleopatra being repainted at Redhill Marina, Ratcliffe-on-Soar in late 2008. [Photo: Mr & Mrs John Marsden]

HMS Cleopatra on the Nottingham Sea Cadet Corps' mooring on the River Trent c 2007. [Photo: Terry Waldron]

HMS Cleopatra moored on the River Soar at Abbey Park, Leicester, in 1973. [Photo: Sydney Harrison]

The stern of Cleopatra, showing the characteristic rudder stops projecting below the counter. [Photo: Mr & Mrs John Marsden]

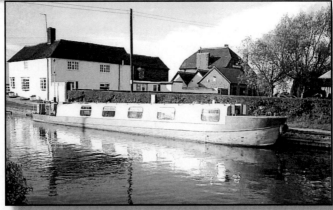

Cleopatra moored at Alrewas, Trent & Mersey Canal, October 1990. [Photo: Harry Arnold, Waterway Images]

The distinctive bow of Woodbine clearly identifies her as HMS London. [Photo: John and Jean Moore]

Web quite early on, and the photographs the Marsdens had sent me of *Cleopatra*, I could describe a number of features that were characteristic of John Pinder's boats for the Navy, both those visible on the decks of the boats, and some that would only be seen when a boat was out of the water.

Characteristic of all the boats were the paired, mushroom-topped mooring cleats at front and back. All four boats had rubbing strakes to protect the curve from the stem of the bow to the full width of the hull, but the number and curved uplift of the strakes was different on each boat. Only *Renown*, the 'submarine' had, under its bulbous casing, a proper flared, Josher-style narrowboat bow. One underwater feature of *Cleopatra*, as I knew from the Marsdens' photographs, was that there were two rod-like 'stops' that projected below the back deck, that were evidently intended to prevent the rudder from swinging too far forward. This was the detail that clinched the real identity of Woodbine. Jean emailed me excitedly:

This is so exciting! John said if we know for sure she is HMS Sheffield *we will have a nice brass plate made for her in her honour - she deserves that. Please keep me up to date with all your news. This is all wonderful and very interesting!*

Two down, two to go!

7.

Target in Sight

By now I was like a bloodhound on the scent. A number of people had suggested that another of the boats had been, or was on the Ashton Canal in Greater Manchester. There was no consensus on exactly which boat it was, but it was worth investigating further.

I had spoken on the phone to Robert Holmes of the Ashton Packet Boat Company, who had a complicated story to tell about a boat called *Minerva* that had been on his moorings for some years, and whose owner had seemingly disappeared, despite having spent a lot of money on having the boat fitted out and re-engined. Rob seemed quite sure that *Minerva* was another survivor of the Canal Fleet.

Terry had emailed to say: *Jim Shead's web pages list all known boats: it gives a* Minerva *as: Built by Warble Boats Ltd / Pinder, 60ft long beam 6ft 10ins, BW Registration No. 71918. If you contact BW licensing and give your name and email and ask if the owner could contact you, then you can ask questions like "Can I have some photos and do you know any history?" The bow shape, height at prow and rubbing strake will tell you which boat it is. The bow heights of* Sheffield, London *and* Renown *are all similar, but the height of the rubbing strake does differ, and there is a difference on* Renown *- the shape of the top of the bow section."*

Despite the fact that the Ashton Packet Boat Company's yard was no more than fifty miles from where I live, so that it would be easy – and potentially exciting – for me to go and test out Terry's ideas about identifying the boat, other things got in the way, as they do. I had made enquiries of the Royal Naval Museum at Portsmouth, in the hope that they would have background documentation on the Canal Fleet. When the reply came it was not encouraging. Heather Johnson, the Acting Librarian wrote:

I sincerely regret I have not been able to establish the exact details of an inland waterways fleet from our collections here. I can confirm that Lieutenant Commander J Green was in post and appears to have been assigned to one of the Defence Research departments (navy) during 1972-73 from the Navy Lists we hold here. However, if the project had been undertaken this would have generated the paperwork the Royal Navy accrues and the best source of that would be the correspondence and accounts from Admiralty Collections of the National Archives. However the period you are looking at may hit the 30 year ruling on public disclosure. If the fleet were in active service until 1978 the papers would be due for release this year, if it was in service later until 1980 (for example) these papers will not be available until 2010 at the earliest. You may find the idea discussed in the earlier papers of the 1970s as a preliminary starting point... I hope this information is of some assistance to you and wish you every success with your research as we ourselves would be interested to know if you locate anything further on this.

Well, if the Naval Museum was in the dark, and even hinting at asking for help, what chance did I have? Still, Terry and I kept plugging away with our research and it was some weeks before I decided to take a drive along the motorway to Guide Bridge to have a look at *Minerva*.

Within a couple of minutes of leaving the M60 motorway, an old road paved with square stone setts led, at first unpromisingly, to a pair of high, blue painted gates underneath which ran what looked like a narrow gauge railway line. Once through the gate and past a few parked cars, a dirt path led down a slope, between a small wooded area and a railway embankment. At the bottom, an area of hard standing, with three railed slipways, sloped down into the dark water of the Ashton Canal.

The boat yard was dominated by a modern green shed, long enough to accommodate a seventy foot boat; Rob led me through the shed where a wooden narrowboat was in the process of being repainted. Outside, two restored wooden boats, an LNER motor called *Joel* and *Maria,* a Manchester, Sheffield & Lincolnshire Railway butty, lay moored up, together with a motley collection of historic boats and some that were less so. The 2 foot (0.60 metre) gauge railway, with a complexity of points, threaded its way through the yard.

Two men were putting the finishing touches to Graham Beard's beautifully restored and painted Samuel Barlow narrowboat *Daphne*, a couple of small boys darted sure-footedly on and off pontoons. A skeletal, jib-less crane poked up above the trees and moored alongside one of the boats was a bright orange dredger. There were signs of much busyness but the atmosphere was relaxed and nothing seemed to be done in a rush.

"What an amazing place," I said to Rob.

"Mmm," he replied. "I like to think of it as a playground for adults."

Two women, who Rob introduced as his wife and daughter, arrived carrying supermarket bags full of food and disappeared into the cabin of a narrowboat that I hadn't really noticed before, which had smoke drifting lazily from a stove chimney.

"So which is the boat that you think is one of the Navy 'warships'?" I asked Rob.

"That one."

He pointed to the boat the two women had just boarded. It was moored next to the bank, hemmed in by a couple of other boats.

Minerva, like *Cleopatra* and *Sheffield*, bore little resemblance to a warship. When I climbed over the taffrail and stepped on to the rear deck, however, there were two give-away signs that this was indeed another of the fleet: the stern was very slightly bowed, not rounded, and there were mushroom-shaped twin cleats just like those on the other two boats.

HMS Renown and HMS Cleopatra at Little Venice. [Photo: TS Hermes]

The Manchester, Sheffield & Lincolnshire Railway butty Maria.

"What makes you think this is one of the Royal Navy boats?" I asked.

"Well, it was the Navy that brought it here in the first place."

"Really? When was that?"

"Late 70's or early 80's I think."

If Rob is right about the date, it must have been brought north from Bulls Bridge soon after the fleet was decommissioned.

"So who owns it?" I asked.

"Now that's a long story," Rob said with a laugh. "How long have you got?"

"All day."

"You'd better come into the cabin," he said.

The cabin was fitted out in some style with a lot of real wood, obviously a professional job. Equipped with mugs of coffee, we sat at the table and Rob recounted the strange afterlife of the boat.

"It was bought by a chap who'd sold his haulage business and was said to be a millionaire. He had it very expensively altered and fitted out by Warble Narrowboats in Hyde, just up the canal from here. He asked me if he could moor it here. It sat on the mooring for ages – I don't think he ever went out on it. He came down one time with his wife, who didn't look impressed; I don't think canals were quite her thing. Anyway, it seems that he'd invested his money in property and lost it. I haven't seen him or heard from him for years."

"So who owns it now?" I asked, because it looked as if Rob had made himself at home on the boat.

"I suppose he does, but I don't even know if he's still alive. And, as you can see…"

"He can have it back when he's paid the mooring fees…?"

"I suppose so. It's a bit of a grey area really."

"Going back to the Navy," I said, "which boat do you think this is?"

"Like I told you on the phone, I've always thought it was *Cleopatra*."

"Well, I can tell you that it definitely isn't *Cleopatra*. By a process of deduction, I'm pretty sure it's *London*, one of the destroyers. The only other one I haven't accounted for is the submarine, *Renown*, but I'm nine-nine percent certain this is *London*."

Rob's wife interrupted to ask if I'd like some lunch. I started to say no, but she said, "We're making it anyway, and there's plenty."

The smell of good cooking filled the cabin.

"In that case, yes. Thanks very much."

So that was how I came to 'mess' aboard HMS *London*, leaving just *Renown* to find.

A little bird somewhere had said that the one boat that still had to be found was moored on the Grand Union Canal "somewhere near Uxbridge", so the obvious place to start was to look for marinas in the Uxbridge area and contact them, to see if any of them knew of the boat.

Of the three marinas I found on the Web and emailed only one – the British Waterways owned Packet Boat Marina – replied. Lynn Halstead's reply said, "I am sorry, but I do not know of any such boat in this area. I suggest you get hold of Deborah Figeuiredo who is the Enforcement Co-ordinator for BW in this area. She does regular patrols and has a good idea of all boats around here".

I felt very optimistic that, with help from someone in Deborah's position, I would find *Renown* in no time. I immediately emailed Deborah, or Debbi as she prefers to be known. I can't speak too highly of her efforts on my behalf. She didn't know *Renown*'s whereabouts, but she pulled out all the stops for me to try to find her. But, eventually, to her evident frustration and mine, she had to admit defeat. Her email, with its ominous subject, "Former Royal Navy boat 'Renown' - no joy", read:

I've just spent an extremely frustrating evening interrogating the current craft records, along with the archived computer records with no joy. The craft were not registered consecutively and I could not successfully identify the Royal Navy customer number either which might have given me the other way of finding it. I've now exhausted every permutation and local boaters have not been able to help either. Sorry not to have better news but we did try.

At least Debbi did come up with a probable reason for being unable to find the boats on the British Waterways register. In a further email, she wrote:

"From my work on the records… I can only assume that the craft were not registered with BW but had short term licences hence no index numbers. I did find evidence of Royal Navy short term licences but, because of the way they are processed, you cannot tell for which craft. It was only when Cleopatra *came permanently on to the BW system with the Sea Cadets that she was issued an index number".*

It did make sense because, as we have seen, the boats were active for exactly six months of the year. It may well have been that, as they spent the winter months at the British Waterways yard at Bulls Bridge, they were entitled to, or granted, exemption from being licensed for the other six months, since BW was in any case earning money for servicing and refitting the fleet.

8.

The Wrong Sort of People

*'The wrong sort of people': a group of children
aboard HMS Cleopatra at Little Venice. [Photo: RN]*

The ultimate question to be asked is 'Did the Canal Fleet achieve an increase in the number of young men recruited for the Royal Navy?' The answer is, probably not. It was a very British, slightly eccentric, even romantic inspiration, and the boats did attract large numbers of visitors – from 1973 to 1977 typically over 200,000 people in a six month period each year – but the sad truth was that they were, by and large, the wrong sort of people.

Perhaps it would be best to let someone who was actually involved with the fleet explain why that was. Towards the end of his career in the Royal Navy, as a pilot in the Fleet Air Arm, the author Charles Gidley Wheeler, by then a Lieutenant Commander, was in his own words, "put out to grass in the Directorate of Naval Recruiting and was put in charge of the canal fleet for (I think) the 1975 season... My London office was under the Admiralty Arch. I was a serving Lieutenant

Commander on the active list at the time but I had fallen out with a senior officer while serving at the joint maritime operational training staff in Scotland… I shared an office with retired Chief Petty Officer Tinker, known as 'Tinks', who visited Harry [Tate] when he was in his last months in hospital".

Charles goes on to say, "Frankly, I think [the Canal Fleet] was a bit of a waste of taxpayers' money, as it was aimed at [or at least tended to attract] children between six and twelve". He also thought that "the interiors of the [boats] were a bit of a disappointment, as they consisted of obsolete pieces of hardware that did not really inspire the young to take up a life on the ocean wave!" To be fair to the originators of the idea, Charles' opinion of naval 'obsolete hardware' was probably not shared by the eager schoolboys who visited the boats; they were not in a position to know whether the instruments they saw were bang up to date or out of the Ark, although a serving Royal Navy officer undoubtedly was. Without doubt, visiting the Canal Fleet would have planted the seed in the minds of some of the youngsters, and they would have gone on to join the Navy seven or eight years later, but what the Navy really needed was recruits right then.

Charles Wheeler says, "With regard to the recruitment aspect: you are probably right that the aim was to recruit teenagers. However, my experience at the three shows I attended was that very few teenagers went through the boats, and that the majority of visitors – the vast majority – consisted of Dads with under ten-year-olds". It is his considered opinion that "The real cause of the fall off in recruitment was that the Royal Navy was being severely cut back, in particular [with] the aircraft carriers not being replaced. I'm sorry to say that I don't think the canal fleet project did anything positive to interest potential recruits".

Like much else in our society, public relations, advertising and recruitment have all become much more sophisticated in the 21st Century, helped not least by the power of computers. As far as Naval recruiting is concerned, it was ultimately the land based Royal Navy Presentation Team that, like a racehorse whose jockey bides his time, has come up on the rails and won by a length.

The model for the Presentation Team is the same as that used for corporate presentations by business, industry, universities and even schools to attract customers, graduates or academic high-fliers. The Team travels the whole of the UK talking to a wide cross-section of the community including business, schools and colleges, local government, youth groups among others.

The Team, of course, makes use of multimedia presentations to illustrate and explain the Royal Navy and its role, its people, equipment and plans for the future. As well as being informative, its presentations are designed to be entertaining. Communicating with young adults today also means that the Team has to expect lively debate from well informed people whose candid opinions have to be dealt with on the same level. An appeal to the patriotic instinct alone is not guaranteed to win recruits.

The Presentation Team's literature says, "Our aim is to convince you that your Royal Navy offers good value for money, and that your taxes are being spent wisely". It is a recognition that, whether through our education system, or the extent to which we are bombarded by electronic and print media, the potential recruits of today must be engaged with intellectually, rather than through their emotions. And yet, it would be pleasing to think that the excitement engendered in the schoolchildren of the mid-1970s by that fleet of little ships which cruised the inland waterways did succeed, perhaps in a longer time scale than originally envisaged, in attracting some of the bravest and boldest to enlist in the Senior Service.

Today's Royal Navy Presentation Team. [Photo: RN]

Bibliography and Sources

Terry Waldron; Nick Wall, Editor 'Canal Boat'; Navy News; Tony Hoyland, Editor, Towpath Talk; Waterways World, May 1974; *ibid* November 1977; Waterways News, May 1973; Hugh McKnight; lefarkins.blogspot.com; 'The Royal Navy 1930-1990: Innovation and Defense', Edited by Richard Harding, Routledge, ISBN: 978-0-7146-5710-3; Michelle Welsh, Lieutenant (SCC) MCGI RNR, Commanding Officer, Nottingham Sea Cadet Corps; Graham Broadbent, Commanding Officer, Thameside Sea Cadet Corps; Robert Holmes, Ashton Packet Boat Company, *Minerva*; Lieutenant P J Saupé, RNR, Commanding Officer TS *Hermes*, Tiverton Sea Cadet Corps, Devon; Royal Naval Museum, Portsmouth; Ministry of Defence, Public Enquiry Office; Colin Edmondson; Brent Hinchliffe; Harry Arnold; Ray, Nb *Owl*, Down Shropshire; Martin Clark; Mike Dowling; John Pinder; Colin Stone; Cath Turpin, Boat Museum Society; Mark Ellard, Redhill Marina, Ratcliffe-on-Soar; George Stokes; Mr & Mrs John Marsden *Cleopatra*; Bob Chapman; Eric Reeves; David 'Tankerman' Brook (pladju. co.uk); Tony Murphy; Janice Wones; Neil Michael Duffy; Sussex Association of Naval Officers; Sydney Harrison; Jean & John Moore, *Woodbine*; David Cooper; Peter Scott; Mike Cole-Hamilton; Charles Gidley Wheeler; Debbi Figueiredo, Enforcement Co-ordinator, BW London; Jackie Hallowes; Lynn Halstead, Packet Boat Marina, Uxbridge; Gordon Smith (naval-history.net); David Cooper; Steve Tanner, M&E Supervisor, British Waterways, Brentford; Rhona Delamer, Central Office of Information; Mike Cole-Hamilton; Heather Johnson, Acting Librarian, Royal Naval Museum.